W. D. Johnston

Slavery in Rhode Island

W. D. Johnston

Slavery in Rhode Island

ISBN/EAN: 9783743321335

Manufactured in Europe, USA, Canada, Australia, Japa

Cover: Foto ©ninafisch / pixelio.de

Manufactured and distributed by brebook publishing software
(www.brebook.com)

W. D. Johnston

Slavery in Rhode Island

SLAVERY IN

RHODE ISLAND

1755-1776

BY

WILLIAM D. JOHNSTON, A. B.

PROVIDENCE

PRINTED FOR THE SOCIETY

1894

CONTENTS.

PART I. INTRODUCTION: SLAVERY BEFORE 1755.

I. THE LAW AND THE SLAVE.

Page

Introduction... 113
Legislation in 17th century.. 114
Results of this legislation ; manumission......................... 114
Legislation from 1700 to 1755..................................... 116
Character of this legislation..................................... 117
White slave and black slave 119

II. THE CHURCH AND THE SLAVE.

Activity and teaching of the Church of England.................... 119
Attitude of the Quakers toward slavery............................ 121
Influence of the church upon the status of the slave.............. 121

III. THE SLAVE TRADE AND THE EXTENT OF SLAVERY.

Growth of the slave trade... 122
Reasons for the decline of the slave trade........................ 125
Extent and distribution of slavery................................ 126

PART II. SLAVERY BETWEEN 1755 AND 1776.

I. SLAVE LEGISLATION.

Laws between 1755 and 1774.. 129
Law of 1774; origin... 130
Character of slave legislation 133

II. SOCIAL LIFE OF THE SLAVES.

The sale of negroes... 134
Social attainments.. 135
Knowledge of trades... 136
Occupations... 136
Care for slaves ; amusements...................................... 137
Election day.. 139
Free negroes.. 141

III. THE CHURCH AND THE SLAVE.

Page

Changing attitude toward slavery.................................. 141
Church of England ; sermons..................................... 142
Results ; education... 143
The Quakers; John Woolman..................................... 144
Action by the Quakers ; sentiment against slave trade.............. 146
Progress of the movement; sentiment against slave-holding......... 151
Other ecclesiastical bodies ; Samuel Hopkins..................... 152
The unorthodoxy of reform....................................... 155
Moral and economic reasons for decay of slavery.................. 156

IV.   ANTI-SLAVERY AGITATION.

Anti-slavery literature... 157
Object and success of the agitation............................... 159
Will of Moses Brown... 160
The movement in Narragansett.................................... 163
Conclusion.. 164

EDITORIAL NOTES.

SLAVERY IN RHODE ISLAND, 1755-1776.*

PART I.

INTRODUCTION: SLAVERY BEFORE 1755.

I. THE LAW AND THE SLAVE.

Introduction. The history of slavery in Rhode Island, from 1755 to 1776, is the history of the decay of the institution in that colony. Anti-slavery sentiment and agitation may be traced back to the time of Roger Williams, the founder of the colony. Moore speaks of "the humane efforts of Roger Williams and John Eliot to abate the severity of judgment against captives, and mitigate the horrors of slavery in Massachusetts." Beside these, several of the leading spirits of the seventeenth century had raised a protest against the institution of slavery, but it was not till 1717 that any organized effort against slaveholding was made, and it was not until the time of the approaching revolution that this feeling and this thought became at all general.

During these years many forces, economic and social, were active, undermining the institution of slavery, and modifying public opinion with regard to slavery and the slave trade. A consideration of these forces and their varied manifestations is necessary.

*The sources of this account of slavery in Rhode Island in the last generation preceding the Revolution are, besides the books and pamphlets referred to in foot-notes, the contemporary newspapers, the manuscript records of Providence (town meeting, town council and probate), those of the N. E. Yearly Meeting of Friends, those of certain churches in Rhode Island, and the Moses Brown Papers.

Legislation in the Seventeenth Century. May 18, 1652, the following act was passed by the representatives of Providence and Warwick :[1] "Whereas there is a common course practiced among Englishmen, to buy negroes to the end that they may have them for service or slaves forever, for the preventing of such practices among us, let it be ordered that no black mankind, or white, being forced to covenant bond or otherwise, serve any man or his assigns longer than ten years, or until they come to be twenty-four years of age if they be taken under fourteen, from the time of their coming within the liberties of the Colony, and at the end or term of ten years to set them free as the manner is with English servants, and that man that will not let them go free, or shall sell them away elsewhere, to that end that they may be enslaved to others for a longer time, he or they shall forfeit to the Colony forty pounds."

In March, 1675-6, another law of like nature was passed. [2] The New England colonies were in the habit of selling as slaves the Indian captives they took in their frequent wars. Rhode Island enslaved few, perhaps none ; still there were Indian slaves carried into Rhode Island, and it was with reference to these that the act of March, 1675-6, was passed. This provided that "no Indian in this colony be a slave but only to pay their debts, or for their bringing up, or courtesy they have received, or to perform covenant, as if they had been countrymen not in war."

Results of This Legislation ; Manumission. What Williams has said[3] of the law of 1652 is true both of that law and the law of 1675-6 just quoted. They were both admirable laws, but they were lacking the public sentiment to give them practical force in the colony. They were the expression of a part of the colony rather than the whole, and that part, it will be observed, was the northern. The principle, however, embodied in these laws, persisted ; masters sometimes gave slaves their freedom, and slaves took advantage of

[1] " R. I. Colonial Records," I., 243.
[2] Wilkins Updike, " History of the Narragansett Church," p. 171.
[3] G. W. Williams, " History of the Negro Race in America," I., p. 263.

it where possible, to secure their freedom. The result was that at the beginning of the eighteenth century there was a considerable number of free negroes. Emancipation became more and more common, and the colony began to fear that it would have to support negroes whose years of usefulness had been spent in work for their masters, and who were manumitted by them when old and helpless. To prevent this abuse, an injustice to slave and to commonwealth, the Rhode Island legislature in 1728-9 passed a law, [1] providing that when aged or helpless slaves were manumitted, security in the sum of not less than one hundred pounds should be given to the town treasurer.

Yet, in spite of the seeming demand for a law, it must be said that these abuses were comparatively rare. Manumitted servants were usually given a small establishment with their freedom, and were generally able to care for themselves. "A negro man and woman, in 1735, by Ind'y & Frugality, scrap'd together £200, or £300. They sailed from Newport to their own country, Guinea, where their savings gave them an independent fortune." [2] With the growth of Providence, many emancipated slaves shared in the increase of general prosperity, and left behind them effects sufficient to attract the attention of the town council. Among many others was "Jack Harris, a negro man, so called," who died December 21, 1745, and left one hundred and forty-five pounds eleven shillings and five pence, much of it, unhappily, in colonial bills; also John Read, who died December 21, 1753, and left one hundred pounds; Andrew Frank, [3] who died intestate, October 6, 1755, and left to the town two hundred and twenty-nine pounds and six pence, besides an old Bible and farming implements. These facts indicate that the position of the slave in Rhode Island, partly because of public opinion as expressed in the two acts already quoted, and partly for economic reasons, was practically the same as that of the apprentice or indentured white servant. The position of the free negro or Indian was determined as among the colonists themselves by

[1] R. I. Laws, 1730, p. 162.
[2] "Boston Evening Post," 1735.
[3] "R. I. Historical Tracts," No. 15, p. 177.

family, wealth and social attainments. It has been asserted, however,[1] that an examination of the legislation of this period will lead one to believe that there existed some jealousy of the negro, and a desire to infringe upon the acquired liberties of the free negro. Let us consider the truth of this proposition.

Legislation from 1700 to 1755. In 1704[2] on account of thefts committed after nightfall, negroes were forbidden to be abroad after nine o'clock, on penalty of whipping. No housekeeper was to be allowed to entertain them after this time, on penalty of five shillings fine. An act of 1708[3] increased this fine to ten shillings. In 1714,[4] slaves having run away under pretense of being sent by their masters and having on this account been carried out of the colony and often lost to their masters, it was enacted that no person should transport any slave over a ferry or out of the colony without a certificate from the master, on penalty of twenty shillings fine ; that all ministers of justice and others should aid in arresting and returning all slaves seeking to escape in this manner. An act of 1718[5] provided that all slaves who should be found purloining or stealing should be tried and punished by a court consisting of two or more justices of the peace or town officers of the town where the offence was committed, instead of in the general courts of trial and gaol delivery as before. There was the right of appeal to the higher court only in case the owner of the slave should desire it and would give bond to prosecute the appeal. In 1743,[6] there was an Act "for the more effectual punishment of negroes that shall attempt to commit rape on any white woman." In March, 1750–1,[7] an Act was passed, supplementary to the acts of 1704 and 1708, "to prevent all persons Keeping house within this colony, from entertaining Indian, Negro or Mulatto servants or slaves : "

[1] Williams, "History of the Negro Race in America," I., 264.

[2] R. I. Laws, 1730, p. 50.

[3] "R. I. Colonial Records," IV., 50.

[4] R. I. Laws, 1730, p. 72.

[5] R. I. Laws, 1719, p. 101.

[6] R. I. Laws, 1745, p. 263.

[7] R. I. Laws, 1752, pp. 92-3.

" Whereas great disorders and Burglaries are oftentimes raised and committed by Negroes, Indians and other impudent Persons, entertaining such Indian, Negro and Mulatto servants and slaves, and selling them strong Liquors and receiving and bargaining with them ; by Means whereof such servants and slaves are induced and tempted to pilfer and steal from their Masters and Mistresses, to the utter Ruin of such Servants, and to the great Injury of the Public," it is therefore enacted, that no one shall sell liquor to any Indian, mulatto, or negro servant or slave, under penalty of a fine of thirty pounds, one-half to the informer ; no householder shall entertain any such without the owner's consent, nor furnish opportunities for dancing or gaming, under penalty of fine or imprisonment ; transgressors (if not whites) shall have their housekeeping broken up and be set to work for the town ; colored servants or slaves abroad after nine o'clock shall be apprehended and, in the morning, whipped, unless the owner will pay ten pounds ; trading with slaves was also forbidden.

Character of this Legislation. None of these laws, I think, indicate that the negro was treated with particular severity.[1] The attempt was made to prevent the numerous thefts which were committed by slaves, though seemingly with little success. A law was also passed to prevent the escape of slaves from their masters, but this, it must be remembered, was as much in the interest of the public as of the master. A poor stranger was always liable to become a charge upon the town, and it was therefore by no means an uncommon thing to return a poor white person to his or her place of legal residence. By this law for the return of fugitive slaves, therefore, no peculiar discrimination was made against the slave or against the negro. It is true these laws, unlike the laws of 1652 and 1675-6, do not prohibit slavery but are permissive and regulative. The interests of the owner of land and of slaves had become important since the opening of the

---

[1] Slaves were never subjected to severer punishments than whites for the same offences, as has been the case in some states ; and they enjoyed the protection of the laws for offences against their persons equally with the whites. — *E. R. Potter, Report to R. I. Legislature, 1840.*

century, and were now deemed worthy of consideration. The laws of 1652 and 1675-6, as has been said, were the expression of the northern and democratic part of the colony ; the slave laws of the eighteenth century, on the other hand, were the expression of the wealthier southern counties, and were based not on grounds of principle but on grounds of interest and expediency. This change was occasioned by the growth of the Narragansett Plantations, and the increase in maritime trade, which centered in Newport. These laws, however, were not cruel ; they simply expressed what were commonly recognized as the rights of the master over the slave. As Williams says,[1] negro slaves were ratable at law as chattel property, and could be taken in execution to satisfy debts as other personal property. He cites this instance :—

"In October, 1743, Comfort Taylor of Bristol sued and obtained judgment against a negro named Cuff Borden for two hundred pounds and cost of suit for a grievous trespass. Cuff was a slave. An ordinary execution would have gone against his person ; he would have been imprisoned and nothing more. In view of this condition of affairs Mrs. Taylor petitioned the General Assembly praying that authority be granted the sheriff to sell Cuff as other property to satisfy the judgment. The Assembly granted her prayer as follows : 'upon consideration whereof, it is voted and resolved, that the sheriff of the said county of Newport, when he shall receive the execution against the said negro Cuff, be, and is hereby fully empowered to sell said negro Cuff as other personal estate ; and after the fine of twenty pounds be paid into the general treasury, and all other charges deducted out of the price of said negro, the remainder to be appropriated in satisfying said execution.' "[2]

This procedure was not, however, peculiar to the legal treatment of negroes. It was not a rare occurrence to sell poor white debtors in similar cases. For example, Julian Welford and Christina Renshen, two women convicted of theft in Newport, not having an estate, were sold to pay the costs,

[1] "History of the Negro Race in America," II., 278.

[2] "R. I. Colonial Records," V., 72-3.

"but they scarcely sold for enough to pay the person who whipped them." [1]

White Slave and Black Slave.   This was the legal status of the servant or slave, black or white, in 1755, as nearly as we can determine.   The essential difference between the white slave and the black was that there was usually a limit to the white man's servitude, and his children were not subject to the same condition of servitude.   The reason for this lies in the cause of the servitude in each case.   In the case of the white, this was debt or crime for which the penalty was transportation with service.   In the case of the negro and Indian, this cause was a one-sided war, with ensuing captivity and servitude for the weaker race.   With none of the same race or family to care for his interests, there would necessarily not result in the condition of the negro or Indian slave, the same modifications as in the condition of the white slave. Accordingly while we find the treatment of all classes of slaves to be practically the same, public opinion among the colonists, and first of all among Englishmen in the old country, did not go so far as to allow condemnation of their fellow-countrymen to life-long servitude save rarely, and so far as I know rarely allowed the enslavement of children on account of the enslavement of a parent, at least when one parent was left to support the children.

II.   THE CHURCH AND THE SLAVE.

The Activity and Teaching of the Church of England..   We will now examine into the relations of the slave with the church, for these even more than his legal status determined his future social position, and a clear understanding of these relations is necessary to a complete comprehension of the social position of the slave in 1755, and the movement of the following years which ended in the abolition of the slave trade and the emancipation of the slave.

In 1730 Mr. Usher, missionary at Bristol, wrote the Society for the Propagation of the Gospel in Foreign Parts : "I have

[1] "Newport Mercury," 1761.

had sundry negroes make application for baptism that were able to render a very good account of the hope that was in them, and their practices were generally agreeable to the principles of the Christian religion. But I am not permitted to comply with their request and my own duty, being forbid by their masters." [1] In 1740 one negro is reported as baptised. In 1746 thirty negroes and Indians are reported as belonging to the congregation, but complaint is still made of opposition from masters to the baptism of their slaves. [2] Masters felt that baptism was inconsistent with a state of slavery, and therefore made strenuous opposition to the baptism of their slaves, not only here but elsewhere.

Dean Berkeley wrote in 1731 with reference to the negro slaves, [3] "The religion of these people, as is natural to suppose, takes after that of their masters ; some few are baptised, several frequent the different assemblies, and far the greater part none at all."

Mr. McSparran, missionary in Narragansett, in 1741, reports that he has begun the catechetical lecture for the negroes, and spends one hour immediately preceding divine service in catechising and instructing these poor wretches, who for the most part are extremely ignorant ; and whether from the novelty of the thing, or as he hopes from a better motive, more than fifty slaves give their attendance. His journal contains this entry under date of August 2, 1741 : " Dr. McSparran catechised the negroes, and there were present on that occasion at church, near about or more than one hundred." In 1743 Mr. Honeyman at Newport reported "an hundred negroes who constantly attend the public worship of God." [4]

The Society for the Propagation of the Gospel in Foreign Parts, already referred to, though owning a plantation in the Barbadoes and being " under the necessity of purchasing fresh hands from time to time to keep up the stock," early began to take an interest in the religious instruction of the negroes,

[1] Updike, 454.

[2] Updike, 459, 463.

[3] Updike, 177.

[4] Updike, 460, 168, 461.

and when they could not send special catechists wrote to their missionaries "to use their best endeavors at proper times to instruct the negroes," and "to recommend it zealously to their masters to order their slaves at convenient times to come to them that they might be instructed." [1] In "an address to masters and mistresses of families in the English Plantations abroad," issued by this society, we find the following: " Let me beseech you to consider them not merely as slaves, and upon the same level with laboring beasts, but as men slaves and women slaves, who have the same frame and faculties with yourselves, and have souls capable of being made happy, and reason and understanding to receive instruction in order to it."

The influence of such publications was undoubtedly great in mitigating the severity of slavery, especially among Churchmen in the colonies. It was through such publications and through its missionaries that the English church materially modified the relations of master and slave.

The Attitude of the Quakers Toward Slavery. The second ecclesiastical force operative at this time was the Society of Friends. They were the first, so far as we can learn, to put forth an organized effort against slavery. In 1717 the Friends' Yearly Meeting Record says : " The subject of slaves considered and advice given that letters be written to the Islands and elsewhere not to send any more slaves to be sold by any Friend." In 1727 the practice of importing negroes was censured ; and by the middle of the eighteenth century the emancipation of slaves had gradually become a matter of action by the whole Quaker body. " Similar attempts in other sects were rather the acts of individuals." [2] Yet slavery was still permitted by the Friends as by other religious bodies, and by the State. This marks the difference between the middle and the end of the century.

Influence of the Church upon the Status of the Slave. Slavery in 1755 was among many recognized as an evil,

[1] Humphrey's History of the Society.
[2] Von Holst, " History of the United States," I., 279.

yet it was permitted; toward the close of the century it was
felt as an evil and was prohibited. In 1755 the slave in his
relation with his master was treated under law as chattel
property. He could be bought and sold, punished or emancipated at the will of his master so long as this did not inter-
fere with the interests of the colony. Yet in his relations
with the State, on the other hand, the slave was more than
chattel property, for he could be arrested, tried and punished
according to the ordinary procedure unless the master inter-
fered, and the master could be prevented from manumitting
a slave where the slave would be liable to become a charge
upon the community. These relations to the State, and especially the relations to the master, were modified, we have
seen, by the teaching and activity of the church. The
church, perhaps more than any other one thing, determined
the *status* of the slave in 1755, economic causes more than
any other determined the *extent* of slavery at this time.

III.   THE SLAVE TRADE AND THE EXTENT OF SLAVERY.

The Growth of the Slave Trade. It is necessary for us
next to ascertain the extent of slavery in Rhode Island in
1755, and first to consider the development of the slave trade,
which determined largely the extent of slavery.

In the earlier history of the colony there was a demand for
labor which could be met only by the immigration of free
labor, or the importation of slave labor. England encouraged
it because it was more profitable to her commerce, and expressed herself as anxious "for the well supplying of the
plantations and colonies with sufficient numbers of negroes at
reasonable prices."[1] The colony engaged in it, on the other
hand, because her merchants also found it profitable for them.
They could get molasses in the West Indies, convert it into
rum in their Rhode Island distilleries, exchange the rum in

---

[1] "The assiento, a contract with the old French Guinea Company for
furnishing Spanish America with negro slaves, was conveyed to the English by the treaty of Utrecht (1713) and assigned to the South Sea Company, who thereby agreed to land 4,800 slaves annually for thirty years in
the new world." *Arnold, History of Rhode Island, II., 48.*

Guinea for slaves and gold-dust, trade some of their slaves for more molasses again, and make after all a very handsome profit. For these reasons the slave trade in Rhode Island grew rapidly during the early years of the eighteenth century.

Previous to this "Barbadoes was the source whence Rhode Island received most of her slaves. From twenty to thirty was the average annual supply, and from thirty to forty pounds each the usual price. No more than these could be disposed of, owing to the general dislike our planters have for them, by reason of their turbulent and unruly tempers, to the natural increase of those already here, and to the inclination of our people in general to employ white servants before negroes."[1] In 1708 Governor Cranston said that from 1698 to December 25, 1707, no negroes were imported into Rhode Island from Africa. That same year, however, the colony laid an import tax of three pounds on each negro imported,[2] and other acts followed which showed that the trade with Africa direct, or by way of the West Indies, was by this time well established. February 27, 1712, because the tax imposed in 1708 had been evaded, "for preventing clandestine importations and exportations of passengers, or negroes, or Indian slaves into or out of this colony," an act was passed providing that masters of vessels should specify the number, sex and names of the slaves in their cargo, and the persons to whom they were consigned.[3] July, 1715, an act was passed to prohibit the importation of Indian slaves, because "divers conspiracies, insurrections, rapes, thefts, and other execrable crimes have been lately perpetrated in this and the adjoining governments by Indian slaves, and the increase of them in this colony daily discourages the importing of white servants from Great Britain."[4] Another act similar to the act of 1712 was also passed, regulating further the importation of negro slaves. This provided that persons importing slaves "shall enter their number, names and sex in the naval office," and

---

[1] Arnold, "History of the State of Rhode Island," II., 32, quoting "R. I. Colonial Records," IV., 54.

[2] "R. I. Colonial Records," IV., 34.

[3] R. I. Laws, 1730, p. 64.

[4] R. I. Laws, 1730, p. 82.

shall pay to the naval officer a tax of three pounds per head. This act applied to persons also, bringing negroes from adjoining provinces, excepting travelers who did not remain in the colony more than six months, and excepting slaves imported directly from Africa. It directed a portion of the income from this tax to be expended for repairs on the streets of Newport. An act of 1717[1] ordered one hundred pounds more to be paid out of the impost duty fund for paving Newport streets. An act of June, 1729,[2] ordered that half of the income from this duty be applied to street improvements in Newport, and half to the building and repair of "great bridges on the main." The impost law of 1712 was repealed in May, 1732, by order of the king.[3] It had been an important source of revenue to the colony, but its effect had been to restrict the slave trade to some extent, and so to injure the English interests. It was for this reason that it was repealed. The result of the repeal seems to have been favorable. Governor Hopkins stated[4] "that for more than thirty years prior to 1764 Rhode Island sent to the coast annually eighteen vessels carrying 1,800 hhds. of rum. The commerce in rum and slaves afforded about £40,000 per annum for remittance from Rhode Island to Great Britain." As the trade grew Newport became more and more the central market. Captain Isaac Freeman, with a coasting sloop, in 1752, wanted a cargo of men and molasses from Newport within five weeks. His correspondent wrote that the quantity could not be had in three months. "There are so many vessels lading for Guinea we can't get one hogshead of rum for the cash."[5] It is probable that the trade in Rhode Island was much more extensive than in the other New England colonies. Dr. John Eliot says: "The African trade was carried on in Massachusetts and commenced at an early period, but to a small extent compared with Rhode Island." Samuel Dexter says: "Vessels from Rhode Island have brought slaves into Boston. Whether

[1] "R. I. Colonial Records," IV., 225.

[2] R. I. Laws, 1730, p. 183.

[3] "R. I. Colonial Records," IV., 471.

[4] "R. I. Colonial Records," VI., 380.

[5] "American Historical Record," I., 316; Geo. C. Mason.

any have been imported into that town by its own merchants I am unable to say." In the latter half of the century Rhode Island still maintained this pre-eminence, and its chief mart, Newport. During this period Bristol also became noted as a slave port, and Captain Simeon Potter, one of her famous slave traders, flourished about 1764; but before this, by 1755, the trade to Rhode Island had begun to fail.

Reasons for the Decline of the Slave Trade. The decline of the slave trade and of slavery as an institution in Rhode Island in consequence, is due to both moral and economic causes. Some historians assert that slavery was wrong and therefore fell; others that it fell because it was unprofitable. In Rhode Island it fell both because it was wrong and because it was unprofitable; public sentiment, usually expressed in religious terms among the colonists, pronounced it wrong; public, and often individual action in this matter, was based on grounds of expediency, profit and loss. The motive of their procedure was moral, the method of their procedure was calculative and utilitarian.

The strongest moral force antagonistic to slavery was that presented by the faith and conduct of the Quakers, who for half a century dominated in the politics of the colony, and exerted a stronger influence upon the thought and activity of the colony than any other sect. It may, indeed, be questioned whether the high moral spirit and endeavor of Roger Williams would not have been without conspicuous results had he not been followed by this Quaker succession. Another strong moral force at work against slavery was that of the Society for the Propagation of the Gospel in Foreign Parts. The activity of this society in the colony, already described, and the reading of the annual sermons delivered before the society, a kind of literature at that time most influential, did much to modify the relations of master and slave, and finally to do away with the system of slavery altogether.

The physical and economic reasons for the decay of slavery in Rhode Island are more important. "The climate was too harsh, the social system too simple to engender a good economic employment of black labor. The simple industrial

methods of each New England homestead * * * made
a natural barrier against an alien social system including
either black or copper-colored dependents. The blacks soon
dwindled in numbers, or dropped out from a life too severe
for any but the hardiest and firmest-fibred races." [1] Added
to these were two other, distinctly economic, causes : first,
the diminished demand because of the multiplication of laboring white people, and second, the diminished supply and the
increasing difficulty in getting slaves, especially good ones.
Captain David Lindsay writes from Anamaboe in 1753:
"The Traid is so dull it is actuly a noof to make a man
Creasy. * * * I never had so much Trouble in all
my Voiges." [2] Increased competition also acted with the
diminished supply and demand to make the risks in the trade
greater and the profits consequently less.

Extent and Distribution of Slavery. These changes in the
slave market determined the extent of slavery in Rhode
Island from time to time.

The following is a table of the population of Rhode Island
at different dates :

	White population.	Negroes, slave and free.
1708	7,181	425
1730	17,935	1,648
1749	32,773	3,077
1756	35,939	4,697
1774	59,707	3,668

Two explanations of this table are necessary. The census
of 1730 did not include the towns east of the Bay, which were
not added to the colony until 1746. This will account for a
part of the increase of negroes appearing in 1748. Beside
this, about 1730–48 Rhode Island merchants had traded
largely to the West Indies, bringing back negroes as a part
of their cargoes, and in 1732 the impost tax had been repealed. The falling off in the increase of negro population

[1] Wm. B. Weeden, "Economic and Social History of New England,"
p. 451.
[2] "American Historical Record," I., 339.

in the period between 1748 and 1756 is due to the fact that
negroes, who made excellent seamen, were often induced by
the masters of vessels to run away and go to sea. Allowing
for these facts, an examination of the table shows that the
negro population increased somewhat more rapidly than the
white population during the first half of the eighteenth
century.

How then was this negro population distributed? "Of the
negroes and slaves in Rhode Island," says Potter,[1] "the
greater part were in a very few towns, Newport, North and
South Kingstown, Warwick, Bristol, Portsmouth and Jamestown. By the census of 1748-9 the town of South Kingstown
had more negroes in it than any other town except Newport. This is also true of the census of 1774 and 1783." In
1774, out of a population of 3,668 negroes, Newport had
1,246, South Kingstown 440, Providence 303, North Kingstown 211, Jamestown 131, Portsmouth 122, and Bristol 114.
Earlier than this "King's county (now Washington), which
contained one-third of the population of the State, numbered
more than a thousand slaves. The census of 1730 gives a
less number, but it was popular to conceal numbers from the
observation of the home government. Families would average from five to forty slaves each. They owned slaves in
proportion to their means of support. The slaves and horses
were about equal in number; the latter were raised for exportation. Newport was the great slave market of New
England. There were some importers of slaves in Narragansett; among them were Rowland Robinson and Colonel
Thomas Hazard."[2] In Newport there were twenty-two still-
houses. "The large exportation of New England rum to
Africa, which in return brought slaves, increased the wealth
of the place to an astonishing degree. There were but few
of her merchants that were not directly or indirectly interested in the traffic. Some forty or fifty sail of vessels were
in this employment, and it was thought a necessary append-
age to have one or more slaves to act as domestics in their

[1] Report to R. I. Legislature, Jan., 1840.

[2] E. R. Potter, Report to R. I. Legislature, Jan., 1840.

families." [1]   Newport was then the centre of the trade, while the Narragansett Plantations were the stronghold of the institution of slavery.

We have now given the nature and extent of slavery in Rhode Island in 1755, as determined by preceding thought and legislation, by existing institutions, and by the development of the slave trade. This discussion has been necessary to a clear understanding of the subsequent history of slavery in the colony. In fact, because of the paucity of material, this is not only a wise but the only possible presentation of the conditions of slavery in Rhode Island in 1755, for of legal records, public documents, literary remains, or private memoranda or correspondence for the year 1755, defining the nature and extent of slavery in the colony, there may be said to be nothing. We have next to consider how these conditions were modified by the different forces and institutions in the few years preceding the Revolution.

[1] Peterson, " History of Rhode Island," p. 104.

PART II.

SLAVERY BETWEEN 1755 AND 1776.

I. SLAVE LEGISLATION.

Laws, 1755–1774. As has been said, negroes made excellent seamen, and were often induced to go to sea on privateers and merchant vessels, without consent of their owners. To prevent this an act was passed in 1757[1] which provided that commanders of privateers or masters of any other vessels, carrying slaves out of the Colony without consent of their masters, should be fined twenty-six pounds; owners of slaves carried off to recover double damages where the master of a vessel shall be deemed to have knowledge of a slave's being carried off; masters of vessels resisting search to be judged knowing of such carrying off. In 1765 another act was passed regulating the manumission and freeing of negro and mulatto slaves. This act provided that the slave freed should procure sufficient security to indemnify the town from charge. [2] In 1770 an act was passed " for breaking up disorderly Houses Kept by free Negroes and Mulattoes, and for putting out such Negroes and Mulattoes to Service." After repeating the provisions of the act of 1751, for "breaking up from housekeeping" any free negro or mulatto who shall keep a disorderly house, "or entertain any Slave or Slaves at unreasonable Hours or in an extravagant Manner," the statute proceeds :

"And if such free Negroes or Mulattoes have been Slaves, and manumitted by their Masters, the respective Town-Councils are hereby empowered (if they shall think proper) to put out, and bind them as Servants for a Term of Time not exceeding Four Years, upon such Conditions as they shall think most for the Interest of the Town : And to commit

---

[1] "R. I. Colonial Records," VI., 64–5.

[2] R. I. Laws, 1767, p. 234.

them to the Work-House until suitable Places can be had for them," and "that the Wages of every free Negro or Mulatto, so bound out, which shall remain after the Expiration of his Servitude, and which shall not have been expended in maintaining him and his Family, be paid to such Servant, unless the Town-Council shall think it most for the Interest of the Town and of such Servant, to reserve the same for the Maintenance of himself and his Family." [1]

September 10, 1770, the laws for restraining Indian and colored servants, and regulating the manumission of slaves in Newport, were revised. Those found abroad after nine o'clock at night were to be confined in a cage, instead of the jail, till morning, and then to be whipped with ten stripes, unless redeemed for a small sum by their masters. In cases of manumission the owner was to give proper security that the subject would not become a public charge, and the free papers were to be recorded. Suitable penalties were imposed for violation of this law, and a failure to conform thereto invalidated an act of manumission.[2] The statute applied only to Newport, where, however, the greater portion of the slaves in the colony were held. A bill was also ordered to be prepared, to prevent the further importation of slaves into Rhode Island, but no action was had upon it at present. [3]

The Law of 1774; Origin. In June, 1774, the most important act [4] yet proposed was introduced into the Rhode Island legislature and passed. It read as follows:

"Whereas the inhabitants of America are generally engaged in the preservation of their own rights and liberties, among which that of personal freedom must be considered as the greatest, and as those who are desirous of enjoying all the advantages of liberty themselves should be willing to extend personal liberty to others," etc., it is enacted that all slaves thereafter brought into the State shall be free, except slaves of persons traveling through the colony, or persons coming

[1] R. I. Laws, 1772, pp. 24, 25.

[2] Laws of 1772, pp. 34, 37.

[3] Arnold, II., 304.

[4] "R. I. Colonial Records," VII., 251-2.

from other colonies to reside, and that citizens of Rhode
Island owning slaves shall be forbidden to bring any slaves
into the colony, except they give bond to carry them out
again in a year.

As we have seen, in 1770, a bill had been ordered to be prepared to prevent the further importation of slaves into Rhode
Island, but nothing further had been done.   Meanwhile, in
1772, the Sommersett decision had been given in England. [1]
"The effect of this decision upon the colonies," says Arnold, [2]
"was to confirm the views already expressed by many writ-
ers, to stimulate legislation against the system, and to hasten
the emancipation of slaves in New England."

At the Providence town meeting, May 17, 1774, Jacob
Schoemaker having died intestate, and having left six negroes
upon the town, it was voted "that it is unbecoming the character of freemen to enslave the said negroes ; and they do
hereby give up all claim of right or property in them, the said
negroes, or either of them, and it is hereby recommended to
the town council to take the said negroes under their protection, and to bind the small children to some proper masters
or mistresses, and in case they should not be personal estate
of the said Jacob Schoemaker, sufficient to pay his just debts,
it is further recommended to said council to bind out either
or both of the adult negroes for that purpose," and "Whereas,
the inhabitants of America are engaged in the preservation of
their rights and liberties ; and as personal liberty is an essential part of the rights of mankind, the deputies of the town
are directed to use their endeavors to obtain an act of the
General Assembly, prohibiting the importation of negro slaves

---

[1] In this case Lord Mansfield decided that the slave Sommersett must be
discharged because there was no positive law sanctioning the institution
of slavery in England.

"The importance of the case for the colonies lay not in the assertion of
the principle that slavery depended on positive law, for the American
statute books were full of positive law on slavery; the precedent thus established determined the future course of England against the delivery of
fugitives, whether from her colonies or from other countries." *Marion
McDougall,* "*Fugitive Slaves,*" *p. 12.*

[2] History of Rhode Island," II., 321-2.

into this colony; and that all negroes born in the colony should be free, after attaining to a certain age."

Of the town deputies Stephen Hopkins was one, and to him has been given the credit for the passage of the subsequent act in the legislature. Mr. Sidney Rider says [1] on this point, "There is nothing contained in the town records to show that Mr. Hopkins was present at the meeting, nor can we find anything to connect him with the passage of the preamble or with the law itself; nevertheless the style is very like his style, and the mode of reasoning is his favorite mode. He may have written it." Mr. Foster says [2] that "at the direct instance of Stephen Hopkins (himself for many years an owner of slaves, though a most humane master), the General Assembly ordained" that slaves thereafter brought into the colony should be free; * * "The letter of Moses Brown to Robert Waln distinctly states that 'Governor Hopkins was a member of the Assembly from Providence, and was the person who dictated to me the following preamble to the act.'" It is probable that Hopkins was an active factor in the formulation, the introduction and the passage of the act. The fact, however, that strong pressure had been brought to bear upon him by the Society of Friends to set at liberty one of his own slaves, that he did not accede to this demand, that subsequent efforts, continued from month to month, appear to have been equally unavailing, that he was finally dropped from membership in the society, and that he did not emancipate his slave until his will in 1781; these facts, I say, together with our knowledge of the state of the public mind at the time, and the restless activities of Moses Brown, lead me to believe that Hopkins was not the most active factor, but that the individual who did most for the passage of the act was Moses Brown. But while Moses Brown, with the assistance of Stephen Hopkins, formulated the measure, the immediate reason for its formulation and introduction was the action of the Providence town meeting, and the reason for the passage of the measure lay in the state of public opinion at the time regarding slavery. Now, as in 1652, we see that

[1] "R. I. Historical Tracts," No. 9, p. xix.
[2] "R. I. Historical Tracts," No. 19, pp. 99, 249.

it was in the northern and more democratic part of the colony that the anti-slavery sentiment was most developed, and exercised the strongest influence upon legislation, first in regard to the slave trade, and afterwards in regard to the institution of slavery itself. Neither to any one individual nor to the colony as a whole is due this act against the importation of slaves, but largely to the economic and moral conditions of the northern half of the colony.

November, 1775, a bill for emancipation was introduced into the legislature. The abolition of the slave trade had been accomplished more than a year before. It was now proposed to terminate the system of chattel slavery by declaring free "all negroes as well as other persons hereafter born within this colony," and to provide for the liberation of existing slaves at the will of the owners by proper regulations. This bill was referred to the next session of the legislature, and it was voted "that in the meantime a copy thereof be published in the Newport and Providence newspapers, and that the deputies of each town in the colony lay the same before their constituents in town meeting, and obtain their opinions thereon and present the same to the General Assembly, at their next session." In accordance with these instructions the Smithfield deputies were ordered by their constituents to make the bill a law. In this same year the amount necessary as security in case of manumission was made one thousand pounds. This change was probably necessary on account of the depreciation of currency.

Character of Slave Legislation. Slave legislation in Rhode Island may be divided into three classes. The first was characteristically in the interest of the master. Laws were made to prevent slaves escaping from masters, and to prevent their being absconded by masters of vessels. The second class was in the interest of the colony. Negroes were forbidden to be abroad after nine o'clock at night, security was to be given for negroes upon their being freed, strong liquors were not to be sold to them, disorderly houses kept by negroes were to be broken up, and a revenue was to be derived from the importation of slaves. The third class of legislation was that enacted in the interests of the slave himself. This consisted of laws regulating and then abolishing the importation of slaves, and laws restricting or prohibiting the holding of slaves. Legislation of the first kind continued until active legislation began against slaveholding. The first and third forms of legislation are accordingly distinct in time, though they are not as distinct in time as they are in form, for even before it was thought necessary to legislate in the interest of the master, two laws had been placed on the statute books in the interests of the slave, namely the laws of 1652 and 1675-6. This fact leads me to believe that the interests of the owner of slaves were never considered of paramount importance except where they were one with the interests of the colony itself. The number of owners of slaves was comparatively so small, moreover, that, although their social influence was great, it could not be expected that legislation would be directed by them, and in their interests alone. The interests of the slave importer and those of the colony were, perhaps, even less nearly allied. Slavery was the life of trade, but it was not therefore necessary that slaves should be brought to Rhode Island, it was argued. So the law of 1774 must be considered not so much a blow at slave trade as a blow at the ownership of slaves in Rhode Island. The slave trade carried on by Rhode Island vessels flourished many years after this date, and slavery itself flourished for a time, but such limitations were already placed upon it as insured its final extinction. There was no emancipation proclamation, there were no distinct slavery and anti-slavery parties, but there were other anti-slavery conditions, economic, social and moral, which made the abolition of slavery in the course of events an absolute necessity.

II.　SOCIAL LIFE OF THE SLAVES.

The Sale of Slaves. The social life of the slave in Rhode Island was similar to that of a servant in an old English family of that period. Our knowledge of the slave's social position and social attainments is derived largely from newspaper advertisements of the time, and from family records.

Upon the arrival of a cargo of slaves they were put up at auction by the master of the vessel, or by some merchant of the town. These auction sales were held at the old inns. October 14, 1766, a negro was advertised for sale by auction, at the Crown Coffee House opposite to the Court-House in Providence.[1] In the case of private sales of slaves the printer often acted as broker. For example, an advertisement in the Providence *Gazette*, March 4, 1775, reads, somewhat facetiously, " to be sold, a young negro girl born in this town, about 16 years of age, very active, strong and healthy. Would do exceedingly well on a farm, is good natured, has other good qualities, and like the rest of the world has some bad ones, though none very criminal."

Social Attainments. Some of these advertisements indicate considerable ability in the slaves, especially the advertisements for runaway slaves. These advertisements were often headed by the rude cut of a black man, hatless and with frizzled head, running. One advertisement in the Newport *Mercury*, November 3, 1761, speaks of an escaped negro who speaks good English, and is " very artful and insinuating." Others may be mentioned : July 9, 1763, " ran away Sarah Hammet, a lusty mulatto slave, about thirty eight, wore a dark colored camblet short wrapper, old grey petticoat very much patched, brown camblet bonnet, is polite, ingenious at drawing, embroidering, and almost any kind of curious needlework." October 16, 1773, " ran away Cæsar * * plays well on the violin."

Newport Gardner was one of the most celebrated negro characters of this time. " In his person he was tall and straight and well formed ; in his manners he was dignified and unassuming." He was a man, too, of superior powers of mind. " He taught himself to read after receiving a few lessons on the elements of written language. He taught himself to sing, after receiving a very trivial initiation into the rudiments of music. He became so well acquainted with the science and art of music that he composed a large number of tunes, and was for a long time the teacher of a very numer-

[1] " R. I. Historical Tracts," No. 15, p. 207.

ously attended singing school in Newport."[1] He could also
write, cipher, and speak French. His one failing in common
with many other negroes was a love for drink.

Knowledge of Trades. In the trades many acquired some
proficiency. The Newport *Mercury*, April 27, 1772, advertises
a negro blacksmith who makes anchors ; May 13, 1775, a
negro who has worked in a rope-walk and spins a good thread.
The Providence *Gazette*, July 28, 1770, advertises as missing
"Quam, aged thirty, by trade a cooper, strayed probably in a
delirious condition, is of a serious thoughtful turn of mind,
and inclined to talk but little." November 7, 1775, "ran
away, Guinea, a clothier by trade, sometimes pedlar of choco-
lat, gingerbread, Indico and sleve buttons." Advertisements
often recommend servants as capable of either town or country service. Advertised wants indicate to some extent the
demand. *Mercury*, February 15, 1773, "wanted two negro
boys from twelve to seventeen for gentlemen in towns ;"
August 7, 1773, wanted, negro from sixteen to twenty-five,
"free from bad smell, strait limbed, active healthy, good tem-
pered, honest, sober, quick at apprehension, and not used to
run away." These advertisements do not indicate a demand
for slaves in any particular locality, or for any particular purpose other than general service. The slaves received their
industrial and social training in the home of their first master,
and if they learned easily and were faithful, were seldom sold.
This fact, together with the fact of the increasing competition of free labor, shows why there were apparently so few
slaves acquainted with the trades, and why in reality this
number became less and less as the population of the colony
increased.

Occupations. In the domestic work of the colonial house-
hold the slave boys were given the errands and the light
service about the house. Some of the families in Providence,
for example, had rain-water cisterns for their chief supply of
water, "but these were few, and it fell to the lot of the boys,
some of whom were negroes, to go with two pails and a hoop

[1] Ferguson's "Memoir of Hopkins," p. 90.

across the bridge for a supply at the town pump." [1]   Another common watering place was the Mooshassuc, which was the only accessible fresh stream.   "The murmurs of ancient inhabitants against the brawls and disturbances of boys and negroes, who, morning and evening, congregated near the mill, with their masters' cattle, assure us that the early days of Providence had a delightful experience of patriarchal manners.   *   *   The annoyance had become so great that an act of the Assembly, 1681, was passed in order to give some check to the disturbances.   By a communication in the *Gazette*, March 30, 1765, however, it appears that the nuisance was still unabated.   The boys and negroes still disturbed the quiet of the Town street by ' riding in droves' to Mill River (the Mooshassuc), every morning and evening, racing as they went, without hindrance from the constables of those days." [2]

In the south country "every member of the family had his particular horse and servant, and they rarely rode unattended by their servant to open gates and to take charge of the horse." [3]   In Narragansett we find that Robert Hazard had twelve negro women as dairy women, each of whom had a girl to assist her.   "Each dairy maid had the care of twelve cows, and they were expected to make from one to two dozen cheeses every day." [4]   Slaves were sometimes hired out when there was nothing at home for them to do.   Hezekiah Coffin writes to Moses Brown, October 29, 1763, " send us word by the first opportunity what the negroes wages was, that we may settle with his master."

Care for Slaves; Amusements.   The quarters of the slaves were in the garrets of the large old mansion houses and in the outhouses.   They were generally comfortable, if we can judge anything from the scanty figures regarding mortality.[5]

The slaves were dressed very much as the circumstances

---

[1] Stone, "Life of Howland," p. 25.

[2] " R. I. Historical Tracts," No. 15, p. 57.

[3] Channing, "Early Recollections of Newport," p. 91.

[4] Higginson, "Larger History of the United States," p. 237.

[5] Newport "Mercury," December 28, 1772, gives the mortality for Newport, 1760, whites 175, blacks 52 ; 1772, whites 205, blacks 51.

of their masters and the nature of their occupations would
permit.   Advertisements of runaway slaves gave descriptions
of the clothing worn at the time as a means of identification.
The *Mercury*, February 23, 1773, advertises a runaway negro
man "Jack, wore striped flannel shirt, buckskin breeches,
dark striped waistcoat, butternut barkcolored lappelled jacket,
grey homemade bearskin great coat, new with large metal
buttons, one pair of blue yarn stockings, one pair black ribbed
worsted stockings, calfskin turned pumps, pinchbeck buckles,
felt hat."   Another runaway negro is described as having
taken with him several articles of apparel so as not to be described by that.   This was probably true of many who ran
away.   For this reason the description of the clothing worn
by runaways cannot be relied upon as an exact account of the
clothing generally worn by slaves.

The amusements of the slaves were like those of the
English servants.   The old corn-huskings of Narragansett
were greatly enjoyed by the negroes.   For these, invitations
were sent out to all the friends in the neighborhood, and in
return the invited guests sent their slaves to aid the host by
their services.   "After the repast the recreations of dancing
commenced, as every family was provided with a large hall in
their spacious mansions, and with natural musicians among
their slaves.   These seasons of hilarity and festivity—sometimes continuing for days—were as gratifying to the slaves as
to their masters, as bountiful preparations were made, and
like amusements were enjoyed by them in the large kitchens
and outhouses, the places of their residence."[1]   Holidays
were also observed by the negroes, often independently of
master or mistress.   "I remember," says Mr. Hazard, "when
on the spacious kitchen being removed from the old John
Robinson house, there were sixty ox-cart loads of beach sand
taken from beneath the sleepers, which had been used to sand
the floor, a large portion of which, no doubt, had been danced
through the cracks by the jolly darkies of the olden time, who
in some instances permitted their masters' families to be
present at their Christmas and holiday pastimes as a matter
of favor only."   Often the distinctions between master and

[1] T. R. Hazard, "Recollections of Olden Times," p. 119.

slave disappeared altogether. "The children of the two,"
says Mason,[1] "grew up together. The ties thus formed were
often stronger than life. The loss sustained by the master
was felt by the slave, and the disappointment of the one was
a matter of regret with the other. And frequently the slave,
rather than see his master turned out of doors, placed at his
disposal the little that he had saved of his earnings. The
servant expected to work for his master as long as he was
able, and when he grew old and infirm he relied on being
cared for by some member of the family. In this he was
rarely mistaken. Those persons who can call to mind the
kitchens of a former generation will remember the old pen-
sioners who gathered in them.   *   *   The slaves took
the names of their masters. When they were ill the family
physician attended them. When the girl who first played
with her young mistress and then became her maid, was
about to be married, she had a becoming outfit, and the clergyman who united the daughter united the maid. And when
at last death claimed a victim, black and white mingled their
tears at the open grave." This care which masters had for
their servants is indicated in a letter which Jabez Brown
wrote to his brother Moses, September 21, 1770: "Your
negro boy Pero was knocked down by a paving stone hitting
him on the back part of the head. He was taken up for
Dead. But by bleeding etc pretty soon came to. He seems
very comfortable, this morning and am in Hopes he will get
about in a few Days, the Affair was perpetrated by an Irish
man a Hatter by Trade, he has Secreted himself for the Present. I shall endeavor to have him apprehended if possible."

Election Day. One of the most interesting social customs
among the Rhode Island slaves was the observance of election day. "In imitation of the whites, the negroes held an
annual election on the third Saturday in June, when they
elected their governor. When the slaves were numerous each
town held its own election. This annual festivity was looked
for with great anxiety. Party was as violent and acrimonious
with them as among the whites. The slaves assumed the

[1] "Reminiscences of Newport," p. 106.

power and pride, and took the relative rank of their masters, and it was degrading to the reputation of the owner if his slave appeared in inferior apparel, or with less money than the slave of another master of equal wealth. The horses of the wealthy land-owners were on this day all surrendered to the use of the slaves, and with cues real or false, head pomatumed or powdered, cocked hat, mounted on the best Narragansett pacers, sometimes with their masters' sword, with their ladies on pillions, they pranced to election, which commenced generally at ten o'clock. The canvass for votes soon commenced, the tables with refreshments were spread, and all friends of the respective candidates were solicited to partake, and as much anxiety and interest would manifest itself, and as much family pride and influence was exercised and interest created, as in other elections, and preceded by weeks of *parmatecring* (parliamenteering). About one o'clock the vote would be taken, by ranging the friends of the respective candidates in two lines under the direction of a chief marshal, with assistants. This was generally a tumultuous crisis until the count commenced, when silence was proclaimed, and after that no man could change sides or go from one rank to the other. The chief marshal announced the number of votes for each candidate and in an audible voice proclaimed the name of the Governor elected for the ensuing year. The election treat corresponded in extravagance in proportion to the wealth of his master. The defeated candidate was, according to custom, introduced by the chief marshal, and drank the first toast after the inauguration, and all animosities were forgotten. At dinner the Governor was seated at the head of the long table under trees or an arbor, with the unsuccessful candidate at his right, and his lady on the left. The afternoon was spent in dancing, games of quoits, athletic exercises, etc. As the slaves decreased in number these elections became more concentrated. In 1795 elections were held in North and South Kingstown, and in a few years, one was held in South Kingstown only, and they have for years ceased." [1]

---

[1] Updike, " History of the Narragansett Church," p. 177.

Free Negroes. We have already spoken of the condition of the free negro during the first half of the century. In the latter half of the century the manumission of slaves was a far more common occurrence, and the number of free negroes was consequently much greater. The most conspicuous among these, beside Newport Gardner, was Emanuel, an emancipated slave of Gabriel Bernon. "Turning to account the hereditary talent of his race, he established in Providence the first oyster house of which there is any record. It was in the Town street, near the site of the Old Custom House of a later day. To satisfy the craving of a thirsty generation he provided twenty-three drinking glasses, four 'juggs,' twenty-eight glass bottles, two bowls, with pewter plates, spoons, and cooking apparatus in proportion. The knowledge which he had acquired during his former service, ensured his prosperity. He was the first of a long line of such ministers to the public wants. Dying in 1769, he left a house and lot in Stampers street (where his wife carried on the trade of washing), and personal estate valued at £539, 10s. His grave-stone in the North Burying ground is as substantial a memorial as those of most of the wealthier white men of his day." [1]

III. THE CHURCH AND THE SLAVE.

Changing Attitude Toward Slavery. During the years preceding the Revolution the attitude of the church toward slavery changed materially. Negro slaves came to be regarded less as heathen and subjects for missionary effort, and more as men, with rights to equal liberties with other men. On this point, the right of slavery, the position of the church became now more clearly defined. The Church of England, the Society of Friends, and Samuel Hopkins' church, were the ecclesiastical bodies most prominent in this movement. The position of the Church of England is best determined by an inspection of the annual sermons preached before the Society for the Propagation of the Gospel in Foreign Parts, and of the records of the same society.

[1] "R. I. Historical Tracts," No. 15, p. 177.

Church of England; Sermons. In 1755 Bishop Hayter preached the annual sermon. After showing that there could be no property in souls, he continued : " Let us administer to them the comfort of knowing, what good things God hath laid up in store for them if they act a right part, in that trying state of labor, in which God hath placed them under us. By thus alleviating their hard lot, and rendering it more easy and supportable to them we shall gain an advantage for ourselves, for it is the natural effect of such instruction to turn the eye-service of slaves into the conscientious diligence of servants. If we are not sufficiently actuated by the spirit of the gospel to be influenced by motives of humanity, let prudential reasons incline us to administer this Christian consolation to our fellow creatures, who are so strictly our property and so absolutely in our power that no one else can take upon him to help them without our leave and direction." In 1759 Bishop Ellis said : " The advantage of making good Christians even of the negro slaves, will also be very worthy of consideration. For in proportion as their obstinacy, sullenness, and eagerness for revenge shall come to be abated and altered by religion they will make better servants : And instead of needing to be always watched in order to prevent their doing mischief they may become guards and defenders of their masters, and there will be no longer any such revolts and insurrections among them as have sometimes been detrimental, if not even dangerous, to several of the colonies." In 1766 Bishop Warburton said in the course of his sermon, " The cruelty of certain planters, with respect to the temporal accommodations of these poor wretches, and the irreligious negligence with regard to their spiritual, is become a general scandal." In 1769 Bishop Newton said : " As it is now generally known and understood that Christianity maketh no alteration in men's civil rights and conditions, but every man is to abide in the same calling wherein he was called, whether to be bond or free, it is to be hoped that the proprietors and planters will be less jealous of their slaves being instructed in the true religion, which will soften and improve their manners, and make them subject not only for fear but for conscience sake, with good will doing service as to the

Lord and not to men;" still, he adds, slavery is to be much lamented.

Results. The results of this prudential reasoning upon the policy of the church in the colonies, and upon the attitude of masters toward their slaves are evident. The best illustration, perhaps, of the effect on the policy of the church, is the well known anecdote of the good elder whose ventures had uniformly turned out well, and who always returned thanks on the Sunday following the arrival of a slaver in the harbor of Newport, "that an overruling Providence had been pleased to bring to this land of freedom another cargo of benighted heathen to enjoy the blessing of a gospel dispensation." [1] In very much the same spirit Dr. Waterhouse said : "To see the negro women in their black hoods and blue aprons, walking at a respectful distance behind their master, to meeting, was not an unpleasant sight on those days." Its effect on the relations of master and slave was similar. In the earlier years of the century, as we have seen, masters were opposed to the baptism and to the education of their slaves. This opposition became less pronounced, in time, and less noticeable, and missionaries no longer made complaint of the masters. Still the number of slaves baptised did not increase perceptibly. The records of St. John's Church, Providence, then King's Church, show that three slaves were baptised in 1758, three in 1759, one in 1760, two in 1762, one in 1764, two in 1765, one in 1766, and two in 1775. The reports of Trinity Church, Newport, show in 1763 one baptism, in 1765 one. In the latter year the total number of communicants was 120, seven of whom were blacks, "who," the report says, "behave in a manner truly exemplary and praiseworthy."

Education. Efforts made to educate the slaves were not more successful. In 1731 there had been a bequest of land and four hundred pounds to build a school-house in Newport. January 9, 1763, the Reverend Marmaduke Browne, rector of Trinity Church, wrote the Society for the Propagation of the Gospel in Foreign Parts, and said that at the instance of the

[1] G. C. Mason, in "American Historical Record," I., 312.

associates of the late Dr. Bray, and with the hearty concur-
rence of the society he had opened a school for the instruction of negro children. This school, he said, was to consist
of fifteen of each sex, was to be under his inspection, and
would, he trusted, answer the intentions of the charitable
persons concerned in it. August 3, 1772, the Newport *Mercury* gave notice of "a school opened by Mrs. Mary Brett, at
her home, for the instruction of thirty negro children gratis,
in reading, sewing, etc., agreeable to a benevolent institution
of a company of gentlemen in London. N. B., satisfaction will
be given to those who may send their young blacks." These
three records are probably made respecting one institution,
but whether they are or not, the fact that masters did little
to encourage the education of their slaves cannot be doubted,
especially in view of a subsequent item in the *Mercury*. This
appeared March 29, 1773, and stated that on account of the
difficulty in getting thirty negro children for the school, the
project would be given up in six months if still unsuccessful.

Quakers. In contrast with the calculative philosophy which
actuated the dominant thought, both economic and political
and religious, of the time, stood the faith and activity of the
Society of Friends. The Friends acted rather upon grounds
of principle than for prudential reasons. They did not ques-
tion so much as to whether slaves should be admitted to
church membership and education, but fundamentally as to
whether they should be free.

In 1729 the practice of importing negroes was censured.
In 1758 a rule was adopted prohibiting Friends within the
limits of the New England Yearly Meeting from engaging in
or countenancing the foreign slave trade.[1] In 1760 John
Woolman visited the yearly meeting held in Newport. "He
saw the horrible traffic in human beings,—the slave ships
lying at the wharves of the town,—the sellers and buyers of
men and women and children thronging the market place.
The same abhorrent scenes which a few years after stirred
the spirit of the excellent Hopkins to denounce the slave
trade and slavery as hateful in the sight of God to his con-

[1] Whittier's introduction to John Woolman's "Journal," p. 9.

gregation at Newport, were enacted in the full view and hearing of the annual convocation of Friends, many of whom were themselves partakers in the shame and wickedness." [1] "The great number of slaves in these parts," says Woolman, "and the continuance of that trade from thence to Guinea, made a deep impression on me, and my cries were often put up to my Heavenly Father in secret, that he would enable me to discharge my duty faithfully in such way as he might be pleased to point out to me.   *   *   *   Understanding that a large number of slaves had been imported from Africa into that town, and were then on sale by a member of our society, my appetite failed, and I grew outwardly weak and had a feeling of the condition of Habakkuk, as thus expressed : 'When I heard, my belly trembled, my lips quivered, I trembled in myself, that I might rest in the day of trouble.' I had many cogitations and was sorely distressed. I was desirous that Friends might petition the Legislature to use their endeavors to discourage the future importation of slaves, for I saw that this trade was a great evil, and tended to multiply troubles, and to bring distresses on the people for whose welfare my heart was deeply concerned. But I perceived several difficulties in regard to petitioning, and such was the exercise of my mind that I thought of endeavoring to get an opportunity to speak a few words in the House of Assembly, then sitting in town. This exercise came upon me in the afternoon on the second day of the Yearly Meeting, and on going to bed I got no sleep till my mind was wholly resigned thereto. In the morning I inquired of a Friend how long the Assembly was likely to continue sitting, who told me it was expected to be prorogued that day or the next. As I was desirous to attend the business of the meeting, and perceived the Assembly was likely to separate before the business was over, after considerable exercise, humbly seeking to the Lord for instruction, my mind settled to attend on the business of the meeting ; on the last day of which I had prepared a short essay of a petition to be presented to the Legislature, if way opened. And being informed that there were some appointed by that Yearly Meeting to speak with

[1] Whittier's introduction to John Woolman's " Journal," pp. 25, 26.

those in authority on cases relating to the Society, I opened
my mind to several of them, and showed them the essay I
had made, and afterwards I opened the case in the meeting
for business, in substance as follows :

" 'I have been under a concern for some time on account
of the great number of slaves which are imported into this
colony. I am aware that it is a tender point to speak to, but
apprehend I am not clear in the sight of Heaven without
doing so. I have prepared an essay of a petition to be presented to the Legislature, if way open ; and what I have to
propose to this meeting is that some Friends may be named
to withdraw and look over it, and report whether they believe
it suitable to be read in the meeting. If they should think
well of reading it, it will remain for the meeting to consider
whether to take any further notice of it, as a meeting, or not.'
After a short conference some Friends went out, and looking
over it, expressed their willingness to have it read, which being
done, many expressed their unity with the proposal, and some
signified that to have the subjects of the petition enlarged
upon, and signed out of meeting by such as were free, would
be more suitable than to do it there." [1]

Action by the Quakers ; Sentiment Against the Slave Trade.
As a result of the words of Woolman, the London Epistle for
1758, condemning the unrighteous traffic in men, was read,
and the substance of it embodied in the discipline of the
meeting as follows : " We fervently warn all in profession
with us that they be careful to avoid being any way concerned
in reaping the unrighteous profits of that unrighteous practice
of dealing in negroes and other slaves ; whereby in the original purchase one man selleth another as he does the beast
that perishes, without any better pretension to a property in
him than that of superior force, in direct violation of the
gospel rule, which teaches every one to do as he would be
done by, and to do good unto all ; being the reverse of that
covetous disposition which furnishes encouragement to those
poor, ignorant people to perpetuate their savage wars, in order
to supply the demands of this most unnatural traffic, whereby

[1] Woolman's "Journal," pp. 162-5.

great numbers of mankind, free by nature, are subjected to inextricable bondage, and which hath often been observed to fill their possessors with haughtiness and tyranny, luxury and barbarity, corrupting the minds and debasing the morals of their children, to the unspeakable prejudice of religion and virtue and the exclusion of that holy spirit of universal love, meekness, and charity, which is the unchangeable nature and the glory of true Christianity. We therefore can do no less than with the greatest earnestness impress it upon Friends everywhere that they endeavor to keep their hands clear of this unrighteous gain of oppression. * * It is also recommended to Friends who have slaves in possession to treat them with tenderness, impress God's fear on their minds, promote their attending places of religious worship and give those that are young at least so much learning that they may be capable of reading."

The following query was adopted in agreement with the foregoing, to be answered by the subordinate meetings : "Are Friends clear of importing negroes, or buying them when imported ; and do they use those well, where they are possessed by inheritance or otherwise, endeavoring to train them up in principles of religion?"

At the close of the yearly meeting John Woolman called together some of the leading members about Newport who held slaves. "About the eighth hour the next morning," says he, "we met in the meeting-house chamber, the last mentioned country Friend, my companion, and John Storer, [1] being with us. After a short time of retirement, I acquainted them with the steps I had taken in procuring that meeting, and opened the concern I was under, and we then proceeded to a free conference upon the subject. My exercise was heavy, and I was deeply bowed in spirit before the Lord, who was pleased to favor with the seasoning virtue of truth, which wrought a tenderness amongst us ; and the subject was mutually handled in a calm and peaceable spirit. At length, feeling my mind released from the burden which I had been under, I took my leave of them in a good degree of satisfac-

[1] John Storer was from England. It was probably through him that the London letter was introduced.

tion ; and by the tenderness they manifested in regard to the practice, and the concern several of them expressed in relation to the manner of disposing of their negroes after their decease, I believed that a good exercise was spreading amongst them." [1]

In 1769 the Rhode Island Quarterly Meeting proposed to the Yearly Meeting such an amendment of the query of 1760 as should not imply that the holding of slaves was allowed. This was an important step, for before this no one had gone farther than to censure the importing of slaves. The Yearly Meeting, accordingly, was not ready to do more than express its sense of the wrongfulness of holding slaves, and appoint a committee to visit those members who were concerned in keeping slaves, and endeavor to persuade them from the practice.

June 7, 1770, the committee appointed at the previous yearly meeting announced that they had visited most of the members belonging to the Yearly Meeting who possessed slaves, "had labored with them respecting setting such at liberty that were suitable for freedom, and that their visits mostly seemed to be kindly accepted. Some Friends manifested a disposition to set such at liberty as were suitable, some others, not having so clear a light of such an unreasonable servitude as could be desired, were unwilling to comply with the advice given them at present, yet seemed willing to take it into consideration, a few others which we have with sorrow to remark were mostly of the Elder sort manifested a disposition to keep them still in continued state of bondage."

An example of the first class of men is to be found in the records of the South Kingstown monthly meeting for 1757, when "This meeting Received a paper of Richard Smith as his testimony against Keeping Slaves and his Intention to free his negro girl which paper he hath a mind to lay before the Quarterly meeting all which is Referred for further consideration." [2] These persons freed their slaves either of their own accord or at the first suggestion from Friends, but per-

---

[1] Woolman's "Journal," pp. 167-8.

[2] MS. Records of South Kingstown Monthly Meeting, I., 82, quoted by Miss Caroline Hazard, "College Tom," p. 169.

sons of the third class who were possessed with the ideas of the previous century were very slow about manumitting their slaves. "One of the Rodmans, a few years later, was in trouble over a slave. He was condemned by his own meeting, but appealed to the quarterly meeting, which confirmed the judgement of the monthly meeting given against him, 'on account of his buying a negro slave,' and 'it is the mind of friends that there ought to go out a publick Testimony & Denial' of the purchaser, which was accordingly done, and a solemn 'paper of frd⁸ Testimony of Disowning' was read at the end of a First-day meeting."[1] Another famous slave case was that of the Rathbuns, which was before the Kingstown monthly meeting eight years. Joshua Rathbun, having bought a slave, is brought to confess his error, as follows:

"WESTERLY the 27th of yᵉ 12 mo 1765
To the monthly meeting of friends to be held at Richmond next

DEAR FRIENDS. I hereby acknowledge that I have acted Disorderly in purchasing a Negro Slave which Disorder I was Ignorant of, at the time of the purchase, but having conversed with several friends upon the Subject of Slavery have gained a Knowledge that heretofore I was Ignorant of, both as to the Rules of our Society, as well as the nature & inconsistancy of making Slaves of our fellow Creatures, am therefore free to condemn that Inconsiderate act and Desire Friends to pass it by, hoping that I may be preserved from all conduct that may bring Uneasiness Upon friends for the future am willing likewise to take the advice of Friends both as to the bringing up and Discharging of the Aforesᵈ negro.

JOSHUA RATHBUN."[2]

This, as Miss Hazard justly says, expressed very clearly what must have been the general feeling of the day in regard to slavery, and sounds like an honest change of heart. Yet half a dozen years later it appears that Rathbun had assigned the negro girl to his son, who had promised to free her at a suitable time, but had afterward sold her out of the colony. He had done this without his father's consent; but the father had not mentioned the matter to Friends. The son was read out of the meeting, and the father advised to proceed against

---

[1] Miss Hazard, "College Tom," p. 170.
[2] Records of Meeting, quoted by Miss Hazard, p. 171.

him. As he did not, the meeting heretofore held at his
house was discontinued, and finally he also was denied his
membership.[1]

This incident shows the untiring effort of Friends toward
the abolition of slavery in its very stronghold, nor did it cease
with a few cases. John Knowles and Stephen Richmond in
1771 "Appears of a disposition to comply with friends rules
in liberating their slaves." Three Friends "discovers some-
thing of a Disposition to comply," while four " Did Shew the
Contrary Disposition." They were informed on the 29th
of 7th mo., 1771, that all who did not free their slaves may
'expect to be Denied Membership.' Two months afterward
a sturdy Friend appeared in meeting and 'saith that he shall
not comply with the Rules of the Society, Respecting his
Slaves to Liberate them,' and he and three others are therefore denied membership. On the "28th of 6th mo., 1773,
Frds Appointed to Visit Slave Keepers made report that they
don't find their is any held as Slaves by Frds and there are
some yt are set at Liberty and no proper manuamission given
therefore said committee are continued to see that they are
manuamitted and make report thereof as soon as they con-
veniently can."[2]

Let us now turn again to the proceedings of the Yearly
Meeting in 1770. We have seen that the committee appointed
in 1769 to visit Friends who were owners of slaves reported
at the meeting in 1770 the completion of their task. Another
committee was accordingly appointed to consider the expediency of making the alteration in the tenth query proposed by
the Rhode Island Quarterly Meeting the previous year. At
an adjourned session the committee proposed the following :
"Are Friends clear of importing, buying, or any ways disposing of negroes as slaves, and do they use those well that are
under their care, not in circumstances through nonage or
incapacity to be at liberty,—and do they give those that are
young such an education as becomes Christians and are the
others encouraged in a religious and virtuous life, and are all

[1] "College Tom," pp. 172–176.
[2] Miss Hazard, p. 176, quoting Records of South Kingstown Monthly
Meeting.

set at liberty that are of age, capacity and abilities suitable for freedom ?" The query as thus read, was approved and recommended to the several quarterly and monthly meetings with the exhortation "that they take care it be duly complied with."

The epistle from this meeting to the Friends in London reads as follows : " This meeting hath been under a weighty concern for some time on account of enslaving and keeping in bondage our fellow creatures, and after much exercise and deep travail of spirit on that account have come to this conclusion that Friends ought to be no ways concerned in importing, buying or any ways disposing of negroes as slaves, and that they set all at liberty that are of age, capacity and ability suitable for freedom."

Progress of the Movement ; Sentiment Against Slaveholding. The next information we have as to the progress of this movement among the Friends in Rhode Island is found in their epistle to the London Meeting dated June 12, 1772. It reads as follows : " We also have to inform that the conclusion this meeting came to some time past respecting the enslaved negro, we are gradually endeavoring to affect, and have the satisfaction to inform that a few friends amongst us have freed them from their bondage, and with sorrow that some have been so reluctant hereto that they have been disowned for not complying with the advice of this meeting in that respect." In 1773 another epistle similar to that of 1769 was sent from the Rhode Island Quarterly Meeting to the Yearly Meeting proposing the freeing of all slaves. It read as follows : " It is our sense and judgment that truth not only requires the young of capacity and ability, but likewise the aged and impotent, and also all in a state of infancy and nonage among Friends, be discharged and set free from a state of slavery ; that we do no more claim property in the human race, as we do in the brutes that perish, notwithstanding it is to be understood that the aged and impotent and also infants and those in their nonage be provided for, brought up and instructed as required by our 10th query."

In accordance with this recommendation the Yearly Meeting amended the tenth query as follows : "Are Friends clear of importing or in any ways purchasing, disposing of or holding mankind as slaves ; and are all those who have been held in a state of slavery discharged therefrom ; and do they use those well who are under their care, that are in circumstances through nonage or incapacity to minister to their own necessities and not set fully at liberty, and do they give those that are young such an education as becomes Christians and are the others encouraged in a religious and virtuous life ?"

The epistle to the London meeting for this year reports the following progress : "We also inform that Friends' labor for the freedom of the enslaved negroes is still continued, and some Friends have manumitted them, others give encouragement of taking Friends' advice to free them, and when there hath appeared unrelenting obstinacy some such have been disowned since last year." The Epistle to the London meeting dated June 14, 1774, was written in very much the same spirit. It says : "By accounts brought into the meeting it appears that several among us have manumitted their slaves since last year, and some encouragement is given to expect the freedom of others, so that we are in hopes that those who have hitherto neglected it may be prevailed upon to let the oppressed go free." Their hopes were not without reason, for by 1782 no slaves were known to be held in the New England Yearly Meeting.[1]

These facts indicate that fourteen years before general colonial action was taken the importation of slaves was forbidden by the Society of Friends among its members, and fifteen years before a colonial law was made against the ownership of slaves, measures were taken by the Friends to abolish it, at once and altogether. The influence of such procedure can scarcely be over-estimated. The strong social influence of the Friends, and the high moral character of their faith and of their activity, both tended to produce a strong impression upon the thought and activity of the community.

Other Ecclesiastical Bodies ; Samuel Hopkins.   There were no other ecclesiastical bodies so well organized in Rhode

[1] Whittier, introduction to Woolman's "Journal," p. 28.

Island as the English Church and the Society of Friends, accordingly other efforts toward the amelioration of the conditions of the slave or toward his emancipation were made by individual churches.

In Dr. Stiles' church at Newport there were, among eighty communicants in 1770, seven negroes. "These occasionally met by his direction in his study where," says his biographer,[1] "he discoursed to them on the great things of the divine life and eternal salvation; counselling and encouraging them, and earnestly pressing them to make their calling and election sure, and to walk worthily of their holy profession. Then falling on their knees together, he poured out fervent supplication at the throne of grace, imploring the divine blessing upon them, and commending himself and them to the Most High."

The most prominent clergyman, however, connected with the movement inaugurated by the Friends, was Dr. Stiles' opponent in theology, Dr. Samuel Hopkins. Some time after the settlement of Dr. Hopkins in Newport he "became impressed with the state of the town in reference to the slave trade. There were some conscientious exceptions, but it was the general employment of men of business, so as to be the source of the support and prosperity of the people. There were more than thirty distilleries in operation, and more than an hundred and fifty vessels engaged in prosecuting the trade."[2] Newport was at this time the most important "mart for slaves offered for sale in the north, and the point from which they were shipped to southern parts if not taken directly there from the coast of Africa. If, too, a Dutchman in New York wanted a few slaves to work his land, he opened a correspondence with a Newport merchant, or if the market was dull in Newport, a portion of the cargo was sent to Boston."[3]

Cargoes of slaves were often landed near the church and home of Dr. Hopkins. His congregation was deeply involved in the guilt of slave trading and slave holding. "On

[1] Holmes, "Life of Ezra Stiles," p. 157.

[2] Patten, "Life of Hopkins," p. 80.

[3] Geo. C. Mason in "American Historical Record," I., 344.

the subject of emancipation, Dr. Hopkins was an advocate for slaves remaining quietly and peaceably in bondage, and diligently and faithfully performing as unto God the labors of their station, whether to masters who were kind and indul. gent, or to those who were froward and severe ; till there might be an opportunity in divine Providence for them to become loyally and with the consent of their masters, free." [1] This opportunity Dr. Hopkins sought to bring about. He visited from house to house and urged masters to free their slaves ; he also preached several times against slavery, between 1770 and 1776. " His sermons offended a few, and made them permanently his enemies. One wealthy family left his congregation in disgust ; but the majority of his hearers were astonished that they of themselves had not long before seen and felt the truths which he disclosed to them," [2] and a few years later, as a church, passed this resolution, " that the slave trade and the slavery of Africans, as it has existed among us, is a gross violation of the righteousness and benevolence which are so much inculcated in the gospel, and therefore we will not tolerate it in this church."

Dr. Hopkins, further, took a deep religious interest in the slave as well as an interest in his emancipation. Soon after his installation at Newport in 1770, he formed a plan for sending the gospel to Africa. After he had matured it in his own mind, he communicated it to Dr. Stiles. About this, Dr. Stiles records in his diary, April 8, 1773, " Yesterday Mr. Hopkins came to see me and discourse with me on a design he is meditating, to make some negro ministers and send them to Guinea. * * * There are two negro men communicants in his church, that he is disposed to train up for this end. The one is Quamine, [3] a free negro, and the other Yamma, a servant. * * He wants, therefore, to contrive that these two negroes should be taken under tui-

[1] Patten, p. 82.

[2] Park, " Life of Hopkins," p. 116.

[3] Quamine had been delivered about 1750 by his father to a sea captain to bring him to Rhode Island for an education. After sending him to school a while the captain sold him for a slave. *Stiles' Literary Diary, April 13, 1773,* quoted by Park.

tion, perfected in reading the scriptures, and taught systematical divinity, and so ordained and sent forth. * * Mr. Hopkins desired me to talk with Quamine, and examine his abilities, which I said I was ready to do." Another record, dated April 13, contains the following: "Last evening Quamine came to see me, to discourse upon the scheme of his becoming a minister. * * He reads but indifferently; not freely but slowly, yet distinctly, and pretty accurately. * * He has had but little time for reading; seldom any but Lord's days. I did not try him as to writing, but he said he had begun to write last winter. He is pretty judicious but not communicative and I am doubtful whether he would be apt to teach. He certainly wants much improvement to qualify him for the gospel ministry, if indeed such a thing were advisable."

The two men, though ill prepared in many respects, "still retained a Knowledge of their native language, and were intelligent, discreet and pious." The two pastors, therefore, finally decided to give them the necessary education, and to this end issued a circular dated August 31, 1773, and signed by them, and distributed it among the churches of Massachusetts and Connecticut. This circular stated that Bristol Yamma was fifty dollars in debt because he had not been able to purchase his freedom under two hundred dollars, that he must procure this by his own labor unless relieved by the charity of others, and that for this reason, both to pay this debt and to support the two men at school, money was desired. To this appeal immediate and encouraging response was made, and the next year the two negroes were sent to Princeton for instruction.[1]

The Unorthodoxy of Reform. Another plan formulated by Dr. Hopkins a few years later, for the colonization of Africa, shows the breadth of his intelligence and sympathies. Yet it is a curious fact that, respecting both him and the Friends, it was the unorthodox party that did most for the slave. The utilitarian philosophy was everywhere prevalent. In the

[1] This project was given up at the opening of the war because of the removal of Dr. Hopkins and the lack of money.

church, it was, quite naturally, formulated in Biblical terms, so that it seemed truly to have a divine sanction. The philosophy of the church was the same as that of the time, it was only the expression of it that was different. With this philosophy, however, Hopkins and the Quakers seem to have broken as the Methodists did in England about the same time. It was, perhaps, their ability to think away the formulas of the dominant party that enabled them to discover what they thought to be a universal right to freedom, and further to believe in it, and act upon it. And, if it is agreed that it was the unorthodox party in Rhode Island that brought about the abolition of the slave trade and the emancipation of the slave, we may go farther and say that it was because Rhode Island was from the first quite unorthodox and independent, that she was the first among those prominently engaged in the slave trade, to abolish the trade and emancipate the slave.

Moral and Economic Reasons for the Decay of Slavery. That there were economic reasons for the decay of slavery in Rhode Island, is very true, but it is also true that before the Revolution these reasons, in part were not recognized, and in part did not exist. Slavery was still the life of trade, many of the most influential citizens and planters still owned slaves, and private individuals often engaged in small ventures in this profitable business. For example, in 1762 a hogshead of rum was sent to the coast and the following receipt was given for it : "Newport, April 24th, 1762. Received on Board the sloop Friendship, one Hogg^d Rum, marked W. H. No. 2 which on my arrival on the Coast of Africa, I promise to dispose of on the Best Terms & Invest the proceeds in Negro man slave and ship back the first convenient opportunity, on the proper account & risk of William Gifford, per me William Hudson." [1]

In spite then of the economic value of slavery up to the time of the Revolution, anti-slavery sentiment increased in force and was throughout the history of the colony so strong that Potter in his report to the legislature in 1840 dared

---

[1] Geo. C. Mason, in "American Historical Record," I., 344.

even to say that slavery was never countenanced by the legislature, perhaps never by public opinion.

But while it was for moral reasons that the slave trade and slavery were abolished in Rhode Island as early as they were, and in Rhode Island earlier than in the other colonies referred to, it was for economic and prudential reasons that the slave trade in Rhode Island was abolished before slavery, and the final abolition of slavery in the colony took the form it did. The law of 1774 against the importation of slaves into Rhode Island affected the slave trade but little. The only real difference was, that Rhode Island merchants sold their slave cargoes in other ports, especially the southern ports, where already the market was becoming much more valuable. The profit still continued to come largely to Rhode Island, if the slaves did not. For economic as well as for moral reasons, therefore, the law of 1774 was made possible. It did not affect so large a class of people as the later law against the ownership of slaves, nor did it affect even that class seriously. Its motive and spirit satisfied the moral demand, its form and letter satisfied the economic. But while this measure was not so important nor so far-reaching in its results, the law of 1784 against the ownership of slaves was quite important, and the forces which determined its enactment as a law were strong and numerous. We must now examine what was more distinctively the anti-slavery agitation which led up to the act of 1784.

IV. ANTI-SLAVERY AGITATION.

Anti-Slavery Literature. Much has already been said of the attitude of the church toward slavery, and the consequent abolition of the slave trade, in Rhode Island. The moral force thus aroused was also one of the strongest influences against the institution of slavery; but there was beside this and in addition to the organized effort of the church, an anti-slavery literature and the voluntary efforts of individuals.

Some of this anti-slavery pamphlet literature was made up of the sermons before the Society for the Propagation of the Gospel in Foreign Parts, which have already been mentioned.

Besides these there appeared in 1762, "Considerations on Keeping Negroes," by John Woolman. "Some of these pamphlets," he writes, " I sent to my acquaintance at Newport." In this paper he says: " When trade is carried on productive of much misery, and they who suffer by it are many thousand miles off, the danger is the greater of not laying their sufferings to heart. In procuring slaves on the coast of Africa, many children are stolen privately ; wars are encouraged among the negroes ; but all is at a great distance. Many groans arise from dying men which we hear not. Many cries are uttered by widows and fatherless children which reach not our ears. Many checks are wet with tears, and faces sad with unuttered grief, which we see not. Cruel tyranny is encouraged. The hands of robbers are strengthened.   *   *   Were we for the term of one year only to be eyewitnesses of what passeth in getting these slaves ; were the blood that is there shed to be sprinkled on our garments ; were the poor captives, bound with thongs, and heavily laden with elephants' teeth to pass before our eyes on the way to the sea ; were their bitter lamentations, day after day, to ring in our ears, and their mournful cries in the night to hinder us from sleeping,—were we to behold and hear these things, what pious heart would not be deeply affected with sorrow ? " [1]

May 14, 1768, the Newport *Mercury* contained an extract from the Boston *Evening Post*. The burden of this article was similar to that of Woolman's essay ; that while seeking liberty themselves, the colonists ought not to enslave others, and that masters ought to do to slaves as they would have slaves do to them. March 21, 1772, the Providence *Gazette* contained an advertisement for " proposals for printing by subscription a dissuasion to Great Britain and her colonies from the slave trade to Africa, shewing the Contradiction that the Trade bears to Laws divine and provincial ; the Disadvantage arising from it, and Advantage from abolishing it, both to Europe and America, particularly to Britain and her Plantations ; also shewing how to put the trade to Africa on a just and lawful Footing, By Jonas Swan, a Friend to the Welfare of the Continent." The Newport *Mercury*, Decem-

---

[1] Whittier's Woolman's "Journal," pp. 38-39.

ber 4, 1773, contained "Observations on slave Keeping, an extract from a pamphlet printed in Philadelphia," probably John Woolman's. September 24, 1774, the same paper contained "reflections on slave keeping," also from Woolman's pamphlet ; and on January 28, 1775, it printed a poem entitled, "To the dealers in slaves." March 4, 1775, the *Gazette* advertised a pamphlet by the editor, John Carter, for sale at the distill house. The title of this pamphlet was : "The potent enemies of America laid open, being some account of the baneful effects attending the use of distilled spirituous liquors and the slavery of the negroes." August 26, in the same year, the following communication was sent to the printer of the Providence *Gazette :* "Please to insert the following resolve of the Provincial convention for the large and populous county of Worcester in the Massachusetts bay, which may serve to show that while America is conflicting for the greatest of human blessings, liberty, the members of that benevolent body are not inattentive to the cause of the poor enslaved African." Then follow the Worcester resolves.

Object and Success of Agitation. Of these pamphlets and newspaper articles it is remarkable that only one treats of the slave trade. The real point of discussion was not the slave trade, but the principle involved in both the trade and the ownership in slaves. If the negro was a man and not a chattel, the only logical conclusion was that he must be treated as such. For years he had been, tacitly at least, recognized as a man, now he must be explicitly recognized and treated as such. A number of times, as we have seen, this feeling manifested itself and resulted in the manumission of slaves by their masters. These cases of manumission became much more numerous just before the war. The records of these are to be found in many town clerks' offices.

March 14, 1753, Obadiah Brown makes his will as follows : "My will is and I do hereby Order that my negro man Adam serve one whole year after my decease and after such one years servis to be free. I give him my said negro Adam 20 acres of land to be laid of on the North west corner of my farm in Gloucester." The will of John Field, dated June 26,

1754, was this : "As to my negro man Jeffery I do hereby order and my will is that he shall Chuse which of my Children or Grandchildren he shall think proper to live with, and so far give him his time as to chuse any of them, or any other Person as he thinks proper to take him—provided, that they he shall so chuse, give Bond to Keep my Heirs, Executors and Administrators from all Cost, Charge and Trouble that shall from thence accrue by reason of said negro, Jeffry's Maintainence, and in case none of my children shall see cause to accept of said Negroe, then he shall be kept and maintained by my executors hereafter named." A will of Casco le Favor, free negro, dated November 9, 1762, reads as follows : "In the first place, I confirm and grant unto my Beloved wife, Judith, her Freedom, willing and requiring that she may enjoy the same without any Lett or Molestation." The will of Richard Browne, October 30, 1765, provides that his girl Phillis be freed after she is forty years old, his girl Sylvia at his decease, his girl Anna at forty, his old negro women not to be sold out of the family, his boy Peter to be freed at forty-five. The will of John Merrett, November 24, 1769, was : "I desire and direct my executors that if my Negro woman, Frank, be living at the time of my decease, a sum of money be given by them to some good honest person to take all kind care of her during her life, that she may be treated with all humanity and tenderness, she having been a very faithful servant, and if my negro man, Tom, may be thought by my executors, of ability sufficient to take care of himself, that they give him his freedom, if not that they dispose of him to a master to his own content, and touching the rest of my negroes that they may be disposed of so that there is good appearance of their passing the remainder of their days comfortable."

Will of Moses Brown. Our discussion would be incomplete without a notice of the will of Moses Brown. This was dated November 10, 1773, and read as follows : " Whereas I am clearly convinced that the Buying and Selling of Men of what Colour Soever as Slaves is Contrary to the Divine Mind Manifest in the Conscience of all Men, however some may smother and neglect its Reproveings, and being also made Sensible that the Holding Negroes in Slavery, however Kindly Treated by their Masters, has a Great Tendency to Incourage the Iniquitous Traffick and Practice of Importing them from their Native Country, and is contrary to that Justice, Mercy and Humility Injoined as the Duty of every Christian ; I Do therefore by these presents for my Self my Heirs etc Manumitt and set Free the following Negroes being all I am Possessed of or am any ways Interested in Viz. Bonno an african aged about 34 years, Cæsar aged 32 years, Cudjo aged 27 years Born in this colony, Prince an African aged about 25 years, Pero an African aged about 18 years, Pegg born in this town aged 20 years. And One Quater being the part I own of the three Following Africans viz. Yarrow aged about 40 years, Tom aged about 30 years, and Newport aged about 21 years. And a child Phillis aged about Two Years born in my Family she having the same Natural Right, I hereby give her the same power as my own children to take and use her Freedom, Injoining upon my Heirs a careful watch over her for her Good and that they in case I be taken hence give her suitable education or if she be bound out that they take care in that and in all other respects as much as to white children, hereby expressly prohibiting my Self and my Heirs from Assuming any further power over a property in her. And as all prudent men lay up in Times of health and strength so much of their Honest earnings as is over and above their needful expenses for Clothing etc so it is my direction and advice to you that you deposit in my Hands such a part of your Wages as is not from Time to Time Wanted, taking my Receipt therefore, to put to Interest and to apply it for your Support when through Sickness or otherwise you may be unable to Support Your Selves, or to be applyd to the Use of your Children (if Free) and if not to the purchasing their Freedom and if not wanted for these Useses to be given in your Wills to such Persons or for such use as you may think proper. And for your encouragement to such Sober Prudence and Industry I hereby give to the first Six Named (the other three having good Trades) the use of one acre of Land as marked off on my Farm as long as you improve it to good purpose. I now no longer consider you as

slaves nor myself as your Master but your Friend and so long
as you behave well may you expect my further countenance,
support and assistance. And as you will consider this as an
instrument of extending your Liberty so I hope you will
always remember and practice this my earnest desire and
advice that accompanys it, that you use not the liberty hereby
granted you to Licenciousness, nor take ocation or opportunity thereby to go into or practice the lusts of the flesh, the
lusts of the eye or pride on any ocation or Temptation, but
be more consious than heretofore and with love serve one
another and all men, not only to please Men but as fearing
and reverancing that Holy God who sees all the secret actions
of men And receive your liberty with a humble sense of its
being a Favor from the Great King of Heaven and Earth who
through his Light that shines upon the consciences of all
men, Black as well as white, and thereby sheweth us what is
Good, and that the Lord's requirings of each of us to do
Justice, to have Mercy and to walk humbly with our God is
the cause of this my duty to you, be therefore watchful and
attentive to that divine teaching in your own minds that
convinces you of sin and as you dutifully obey the enlighten-
ings and teachings it will not only cause you to avoid pro-
faneness and wickedness, as stealing, lying, swearing, drinking, lusting after women, frolicking and the like sinful courses
but will teach you and lead you into all that is necessary for
you to know, as your duty to the great master of all men, for
he has said respecting mankind—universally, I will put my
law into their inward parts, and write it in their hearts and
they shall All Know me from the least, to the greatest, and
therefore you can't plead ignorance that you don't know your
duty to the God that made you, because you can't all read his
mind and will in the scriptures, which is indeed a great Favor
and Blessing to them that can understand and obey. But
there is a Book within you that is not confined to the English or any language, and as you silently and reverently wait
for its openings and instantly it will teach you and you will
be enabled to understand its language and as you are careful
to be obedient thereto and often silently read it, you will be
able to speak its language with African as well as English
tongues to your poor Fellow countrymen To the glory of

him who has wrought your deliverance from slavery to whose gracious care and protection I commit and fervently recommend you and bid you farewell." [1]

The occasion of this will of Moses Brown, as well as its nature, is curious. It was after "returning from the grave of his wife, and meditating upon the Lord's mercies and favors, and seeking to know what the Divine will was concerning him;" he says, "I saw my slaves with my spiritual eyes as plainly as I see you now, and it was given me as clearly to understand that the sacrifice that was called for of my hand was to give them their liberty." [2]

Another will, dated August 1, 1775, made by Eve Bernon, provides for the emancipation of her woman Amey, and the latter's son Marmy, and their keep in case they become disabled through sickness or otherwise.

The Movement in Narragansett. These manumissions we have recorded were mostly confined to Providence. There were also manumissions, as we have seen, in the cases of Friends in Newport and in the Narragansett country. Thomas Hazard, "perhaps the first man of much influence in New England," says his biographer, "who labored in behalf of the African race, when a young man on coming home from college was set by his father to oversee the negroes whilst they were engaged under a scorching sun in cultivating a field of corn. As he sat reading in the shade of a tree his mind went out in sympathy toward the poor slaves who were thus forced to labor for others in the heat of the sun, when he himself could scarcely keep comfortable while quietly sitting in the shade. This led to a train of thought that finally resulted in a conviction that it was wrong to hold slaves," and when he was being established by his father he refused the slaves that were offered him. [3]

A similar anecdote is told of another Narragansett magnate, Rowland Robinson : " Previous to establishing his house-

[1] Probate Records, VI., 73.

[2] Augustine Jones, "Moses Brown: a Sketch," p. 13.

[3] "Recollections of Olden Times," T. R. Hazard, p. 102. Miss Caroline Hazard, "College Tom," pp. 42-44, gives another story of the causes of his conversion.

hold Mr. Robinson engaged with others of his friends in sending a vessel from Franklin Ferry to the Guinea coast for slaves, out of his portion of which he proposed to select most of his domestic servants and farming hands and dispose of the remainder by sale as was the custom in those days. Up to the time of the return of the vessel—such was the force of education and habit—the cruelty and injustice involved in the slave trade seemed never to have entered Mr. Robinson's mind, but now when he saw the forlorn, woebegone looking men and women disembarking, some of them too feeble to stand alone, the enormity of his offence against humanity presented itself so vividly to his susceptible mind that he wept like a child, nor would he consent that a single slave that fell to his share—twenty-eight in all—should be sold, but took them all to his own house, where though held in servitude they were kindly cared for." [1]

Conclusion. These were the conditions and the modifications of slavery in Rhode Island during a part of the last century. We have seen that the church largely determined the *status* of the slave, and that the economic conditions of the colony determined the *extent* of slavery. We have seen the growth of the sentiment against slavery, and its first result in the abolition of the slave trade. In the next few years this sentiment was strengthened by the anti-slavery agitation in England and the other colonies, and by the revolutionary spirit, and in 1784 an act was passed which provided that all children born of slave mothers after the first of March should be free, and that the introduction of slaves for sale upon any pretext whatever should be forbidden. [2]

---

[1] "Recollections of Olden Times," T. R. Hazard, p. 121.

Higginson's version of this story is as follows: "Rowland Robinson, said impulsively one day, ' I have not servants enough, fetch me some from Guinea.' Upon this the master of a small packet of 20 tons belonging to Mr. Robinson, fitted her out at once, set sail for Guinea and brought home eighteen slaves, one of whom was a King's son. His employer burst into tears on their arrival, his order not having been seriously given." *Larger History of the United States, pp. 237-8.*

[2] Rhode Island's legislation respecting slavery in the period from 1775 to 1785 has been treated in an essay by Dr. Jeffrey R. Brackett, entitled "The Status of the Slave, 1775-1789," in a volume of "Essays in the Constitutional History of the United States," edited by Professor J. F. Jameson.

EDITORIAL NOTES.

A desire has been expressed that an opportunity be furnished through the medium of this publication to solicit and secure information on certain subjects that are clearly within the scope and aims of this Society. In response to this request, which is largely represented by persons interested in genealogical pursuits, a few pages will hereafter be devoted to Notes and Queries. The usefulness and success of this department of the Quarterly will depend on the practical manifestations of interest in the experiment.

The next number of the publication will contain: 1. A copy of an original communication, dated Newport, June 18, 1787, and signed by eminent citizens of this State, at that period in its history. This is taken from a file of papers known as "The Archives of the Federal Convention." 2. A letter from Dr. Benjamin Waterhouse, written at Newport, September 14, 1822, and addressed to Thomas Jefferson. 3. Copies of certain Military Records of Rhode Island during a portion of the Revolutionary period. 4. Some genealogical notes by Mr. John O. Austin; and probably some similar contributions from other sources.

www.ingramcontent.com/pod-product-compliance
Lightning Source LLC
Chambersburg PA
CBHW030719110426
42739CB00030B/998